OUR

IRISH GRANNIES'

RECIPES

OUR

IRISH
GRANNIES'
RECIPES

EDITED BY
EOIN PURCELL

This publication is designed to provide accurate and authoritative information in regard to the subject matter covered. It is sold with the understanding that the publisher is not engaged in rendering legal, accounting, or other professional service. If legal advice or other expert assistance is required, the services of a competent professional person should be sought.—*From a Declaration of Principles Jointly Adopted by a Committee of the American Bar Association and a Committee of Publishers and Associations*

All brand names and product names used in this book are trademarks, registered trademarks, or trade names of their respective holders. Sourcebooks, Inc., is not associated with any product or vendor in this book.

Some recipes contained herein may call for raw or undercooked eggs. Please consult with your physician prior to consumption.

Published by Sourcebooks, Inc.
P.O. Box 4410, Naperville, Illinois 60567-4410
(630) 961-3900
Fax: (630) 961-2168
www.sourcebooks.com

Originally published in the UK in 2008 by Mercier Press.

Library of Congress Cataloging-in-Publication data is on file with the publisher.

Printed and bound in the United States of America.
BG 11

~◉ CONTENTS ◉~

WHY OUR GRANNIES' RECIPES?

I like food and I love baking. I also love books. So, as a publisher, one of the most exciting things for me to work on is a cookbook. When it was decided that Mercier would publish a book of traditional Irish recipes collected from around the country, the recipes that our grandmothers, mothers, fathers, and grandfathers cooked for us when we were young (or even when we were older and just home for some spoiling), I wanted in.

We thought about how we could compile the list of those favorites, whether they were for pies, casseroles, stews, breads, soups, roasts, custards, scones, cakes, biscuits, ice cream, or any other dishes. We realized that we would use the Internet. Thus was born OurGranniesRecipes.com

The site helps us gather together the recipes that have been favorites of Irish families for generations. In creating this book, we have used recipes submitted to the site by ordinary people, chefs, aunts, uncles, grandchildren, and even a few grannies.

For me, that favorite recipe is for the Apple Tart made for me by my father's mother, Agnes Purcell, née Hourigan (and, after Agnes sadly passed away, her sister, my great-aunt Eileen Hourigan, made it for me, too). You'll find that recipe in here along with eighty or so other recipes, sweet and savory.

I really hope that the book delights you as it has me and provides a source of culinary inspiration for generations to come.

Eoin Purcell
Site & Book Editor

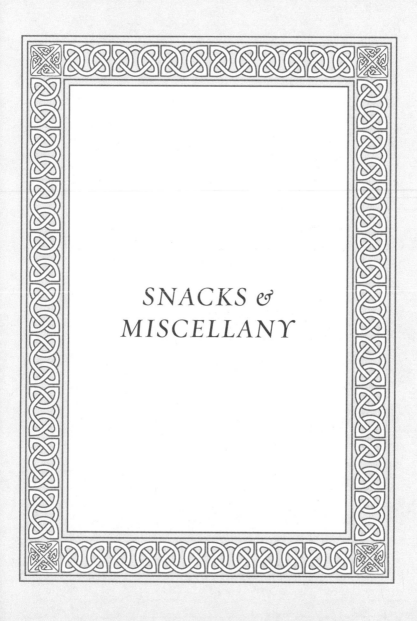

SNACKS & MISCELLANY

INVALID'S BREAD PUDDING

INGREDIENTS

1 tablespoon breadcrumbs
1 cup milk
1 teaspoon butter
1 teaspoon sugar
1 egg

METHOD

Boil the milk and butter together.

Pour over the breadcrumbs.

Add the sugar.

Beat the egg, add a few teaspoons of the hot milk, and stir together, then slowly add back to the other ingredients.

Bake in a small greased pie tin for 30 minutes at medium heat.

JAM SAUCE

INGREDIENTS

2 tablespoons raspberry jam

1½ teaspoons lemon juice

½ pint water

METHOD

Boil all ingredients together well for 10 minutes.

Strain and serve 'round puddings.

APPLE SAUCE

INGREDIENTS

3 pounds apples, cored and peeled

½ pound sugar

1 ounce gelatin

Juice and peel of 1 lemon

METHOD

Stew the apples with the lemon for ½ hour.

Pass them through a sieve, then add the gelatin and sugar.

Pour into a bowl and allow to cool.

OLD-FASHIONED ORANGE MARMALADE

INGREDIENTS

6 Seville oranges
1 lemon
Sugar (see recipe)

METHOD

Wash the fruit well in cold water.

Dry fruits carefully, then slice very thinly and mash them into a pulp, removing the seeds.

Place the seeds in a cup of water.

Weigh the fruit and place it in a bowl of water, allowing 3 pints of water for each pound of fruit pulp.

Allow both the pulp/water and seeds/water to stand for 24 hours.

The following day, remove the steeped oranges from the water and place in a pressure cooker. Strain the water from the pips and add to the oranges. Boil the mix until the fruit is so tender it can be easily pierced.

Take a fresh measure and add 1 pound of sugar for every pint of pulp you have. Return to the pressuring pan and boil until the mix jellies easily when cooled on a cold plate.

For a less sweet preserve, use less sugar.

Pour into jars and cover.

A note from a marmalade fan

The marmalade really needs to be boiled for at least 1½ hours to preserve properly and the jars MUST be airtight!

GRANNY KAY'S STUFFED TOMATO

INGREDIENTS

- 4–6 tomatoes (depending on number of servings)
- 2 cups breadcrumbs
- 1 onion (diced)
- 1 clove garlic, minced
- 10 ounces grated cheddar cheese

METHOD

Slice the tops off the tomatoes and scoop out the insides.

Mix these in a bowl with the other ingredients.

Replace the insides of each tomato with the mix.

Bake in a warm oven for 15 to 20 minutes.

A note from the cook

My granny used to make these as tea-time treats and they always went over well. Warm tomato was always delicious.

GRANNY McKENNA'S COLESLAW

INGREDIENTS

The coleslaw mix:

- ½ head white cabbage
- 1 large or 2 small carrots
- 3 tablespoons mayonnaise (I use Hellmann's mayo but you may like to make your own)

Mayonnaise:

- 1 egg
- Juice of ½ lemon
- 1 teaspoon Dijon mustard
- 7 ounces sunflower oil

METHOD

Coleslaw

Core the cabbage and slice thinly or use a food processor—same for carrot.

Place cabbage and carrot in a bowl and mix well.

Then add 3 tablespoons of the mayonnaise and mix very well. Add a little more if the mix is too dry.

Mayonnaise

Place egg yolk, mustard, and lemon juice in a bowl and whisk together until well combined.

While still whisking, very slowly add the oil.

Continue whisking until all the oil has been added and it thickens.

Then add egg white and whisk quickly.

GRANNY'S NORTHERN IRISH STUFFING

From Koraley Northen

INGREDIENTS

White bread crumbs
Hot mashed potatoes
Butter
Fresh parsley and thyme
Salt and pepper

METHOD

By volume, use about ⅔ bread crumbs to ⅓ mashed potatoes.

Mash the potatoes without milk and add loads of finely chopped parsley and thyme until the mixture is speckled quite green throughout. Add this to the crumbs, season to taste, and work in lots of butter with your hands until the texture feels soft.

This is very light and fluffy when cooked and even improves after spending the night in the cooked bird.

A note from Koraley

It tastes simply wonderful with chicken or turkey.

NANNY'S SIMPLE POTATO CAKES

Submitted by Sharon Collins from Meath

INGREDIENTS

Cold mashed potatoes, preferably left over from the day before

Flour (depending on the amount of potato; for every teacup of potato Nanny used about a half teacup of flour)

Butter to fry them in

METHOD

Mash the spuds with the heel of a cup and keep adding flour till you have a crumbly dough that you can roll out to about ¼ inch thick.

Roll into a round and then cut into triangles and fry them in butter in a heavy iron frying pan.

They should go a bit black. That's OK, though—they taste fab.

A note from Sharon

My Nanny in County Offaly taught me this recipe, and she would make spud bread for us when we went down to see her for holidays. To serve these, she would split them through the middle with a thread and put a knob of butter in each one so it melted and was yummy. We had these with the fry on a Sunday in her kitchen. Serve with bacon and eggs and black pudding!

GRAND-AUNT NELL'S BEEF TEA

Submitted by Grannymar (Marie Parker)

INGREDIENTS (ENOUGH FOR 2 HELPINGS)

14 ounces shin, flank, or skirt of beef
1 pint water
Pinch of salt

METHOD

Preheat oven to 285°F.

Wipe the meat and trim off all visible fat; cut into ¾ inch cubes.

Put the meat into an ovenproof casserole or basin, and add the water and salt. Cover the container with a lid, and cook in the oven for 3 hours.

Strain the liquid through muslin or a fine sieve, and allow to cool. Discard beef.

Skim any fat from the top.

Reheat, without boiling, and serve as a light soup or beverage, with toast or dry biscuits.

A Note from Grannymar (Marie Parker)

Grand-aunt Nell (1894–1997) gave me this recipe about thirty years ago. It was a regular for invalid cookery or nursing mothers.

MY GRAM FROM COUNTY MAYO USED TO CALL THIS...POOR MAN'S FARE

Submitted by Anonymous

INGREDIENTS

3–4 pieces bacon

2 cups chopped onion

1 cup cream

Black pepper

2 potatoes, mashed

METHOD

Chop and fry 3 or 4 pieces of bacon.

Add in your 2 cups of chopped onions to the bacon fat.

Cook until the onions are softened and then pour a cup of "top milk" (cream) on top with a good sprinkle of black pepper.

Finally, pour over rough mashed potato.

A Note from Anonymous

To be accompanied with the remark: "'Twill fill a hole!"

FISH CROQUETTES

INGREDIENTS

¾ pound cold cooked fish
1 ounce flour
½ cup milk
1 egg, beaten
Breadcrumbs
1 sprig parsley

METHOD

Remove all skin and bone from the fish and flake it finely.

Make a paste with the milk and flour and season it nicely.

Mix the fish and paste together.

Form into croquettes, then coat with egg and breadcrumbs.

Shallow or deep-fry until golden brown and serve garnished with the parsley.

GLAZED SAUSAGE ROLLS

INGREDIENTS

A batch of pastry
6 uncooked sausages

METHOD

Cut the pastry into small squares.

Cut the sausages in halves and place one on the side of each square.

Fold the square across over the sausage and seal with a little water.

Bake in a medium oven until nicely cooked.

A few minutes before removing them, brush the tops with a little beaten egg to give nice glazed look.

CHICKEN CROQUETTES

INGREDIENTS

3 ounces cooked chicken

1 ounce cooked ham

½ ounce butter

¼ ounce flour

2 ounces stock or milk

Parsley

Egg

Breadcrumbs

METHOD

Chop the chicken and ham finely.

Make a sauce with the butter, flour, and stock or milk.

Put in the chicken and ham and add some parsley.

Form into croquettes, then coat with egg and breadcrumbs.

Shallow or deep fry until golden brown.

MARY'S VEGETABLE SAUSAGE

INGREDIENTS

3 onions

3 carrots

2 parsnips

½ pint peas

Parsley, pepper, and salt to taste

2 eggs

8 ounces breadcrumbs

METHOD

Boil the carrots, onions, and parsnips, then chop them up very small when cooked.

Cook the peas and pound them when they are cooked. Mix all the vegetables together.

Add in the parsley, salt, and pepper to flavor.

Add in the eggs and breadcrumbs and mix thoroughly.

Roll into pieces about the size of a normal sausage and dip in beaten egg and breadcrumbs.

Fry and serve.

A note from the editor

I was really surprised by this one. Who would have thought vegetarianism was in vogue in Ireland in the past?

A NICE POTATO BAKE

INGREDIENTS

6 large potatoes
8 ounces cheddar cheese

METHOD

Boil, peel, and mash the potatoes.

Line a baking dish with butter, then layer half the mashed potatoes in it.

Grate the cheese and layer half of it over the bottom layer of mash.

Build a second layer of mash before layering the last of the cheese on top.

Bake for about 20 minutes in a medium oven.

GRANNY MURPHY'S MUSHROOM TOAST

INGREDIENTS

½ ounce butter

¼ pound mushrooms, diced

2 eggs

Pepper

Salt

Cayenne pepper

Small rounds of toast

METHOD

Melt the butter in a pan and add the mushrooms.

Fry for 3 minutes, then add the eggs and seasoning while stirring over a gentle heat.

Pile a small portion on each slice of toast.

Garnish with parsley and serve.

YORKSHIRE PUDDINGS

INGREDIENTS

6 ounces flour
1 pint milk
Pinch of salt
2 eggs

METHOD

Mix the flour, milk, and salt gradually.

Beat the yolks and whites of the egg separately, then add them to the mix.

Pour into baking tray with a good supply of hot dripping.

Bake in a warm oven for 25 to 30 minutes.

YORKSHIRE RELISH

INGREDIENTS

1 ounce peppercorns

½ ounce cloves

¼ ounce cayenne pepper

2 ounces salt

½ pound Demerara sugar

Water

METHOD

Place the ingredients in a pot and cover with water.

Boil the ingredients together for 20 minutes.

Strain through a sieve and store in a vinegar bottle.

GRANNY LILY'S SCRAMBLED EGG WITH PARSLEY

Submitted by Roger Brannigan

INGREDIENTS

1 or 2 eggs
Pepper and salt to taste
A little milk
A little parsley

METHOD

Heat a pan and melt a small knob of butter in it.

Mix your eggs with a little milk, parsley, and salt and pepper to taste.

Pour the mix into the pan and stir well until it is set to your taste.

Lily's notes

Most people overcook scrambled eggs, but there is no real concern if they remain a little soft and moist. Whether you like it dry or moist, scrambled eggs are never the same without hot buttered toast.

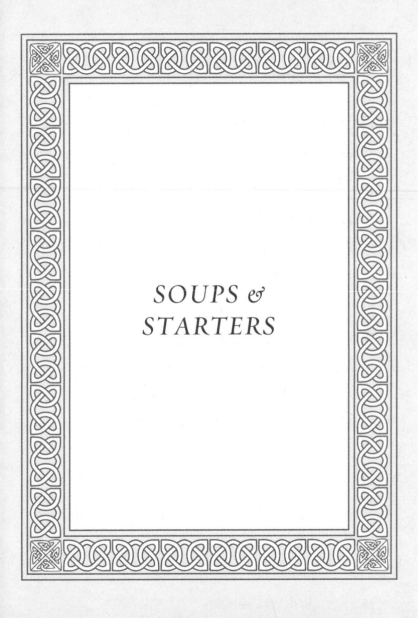

SOUPS &
STARTERS

PARSNIP STARTER

INGREDIENTS

3 or 4 parsnips
Milk to cover
Salt to taste
Knob of butter
Peppers to season

METHOD

Slice the parsnips and lay them in a baking tray.

Pour over enough milk to cover them.

Season the dish with salt, butter, and some sliced peppers.

Bake until browned and soft.

A SPECIAL LENTIL SOUP

INGREDIENTS

¼ pound lentils

1½ pints cold water

1 onion

1 carrot

1 turnip

2 stalks celery

1 ounce butter or dripping

1 ounce flour

½ pint milk

Salt and pepper to flavor

METHOD

Wash the lentils and add the other vegetables (sliced as you wish) to the water.

Boil until the lentils are soft (usually about 1½ hours).

Sieve the mix and blend in the butter and flour together over the heat.

Slowly add the milk to the soup, bringing it gradually to the boil.

Season to taste and serve.

PHIL YOUNG'S GRAN'S POTATO SOUP

Submitted by Phil Young

INGREDIENTS

4 large potatoes

2 onions, chopped

3 sticks celery, chopped

2 tablespoons butter

1 cup milk

1 cup chicken broth

½ teaspoon paprika

¼ teaspoon pepper

METHOD

Peel and dice the potatoes.

Put the potatoes, onions, and celery into a heavy pot, with enough boiling water to cover.

Add a pinch of salt, cover, and cook until tender.

Drain and press through a sieve.

Add the butter and return to the heat.

Add enough milk and broth to reach the desired consistency.

Add pepper, paprika, and salt (if needed).

Simmer for 10 to 15 minutes.

Serves 4.

A Note from Phil

A cheap and nourishing soup to put hair on your chest on a cold day, as my Gran used to say!

RACHEL'S GRANNY'S SIMPLE POTATO SOUP

INGREDIENTS

1 pound potatoes

1 onion

1 ounce butter

1 quart stock or water

½ pint milk

METHOD

Peel and cut the potatos and onion.

Put them in a saucepan containing melted butter.

Stir the vegetables on the heat for five minutes without browning before adding the stock or water.

Bring to the boil and hold there until the vegetables are tender.

Pass soup through a sieve and return to the saucepan.

Stir until smooth and then add the milk.

Season to taste and serve when nice and hot.

GREAT AUNT AGNES'S SALAD

Submitted by Martin Dwyer

INGREDIENTS

1 large chicken

6 ounces bacon

1 head celery

8 ounces grapes (seedless for convenience, red for appearance)

Mayonnaise

3 egg yolks

10 ounces sunflower oil

1 tablespoon lemon juice

Salt and pepper

METHOD

Cover the chicken with cold water in a large pot and bring it to a rolling boil. Let it boil for about 10 minutes, and then take it off the heat and let the chicken cool in the water. (This method of cooking keeps the chicken beautifully moist.) When cool, drain the chicken of the stock (keep this in the freezer for soup) and then take the chicken off the bone and discard the bones and the skin. Chop the meat up roughly.

Cut the bacon into little pieces and fry in a hot pan until brown and crispy. Drain well on kitchen paper and add to the chicken.

Cut the celery into small pieces and add to the chicken. Halve the grapes and discard the seeds and add them in.

Beat the yolks up well with the lemon and seasoning and then dribble in the oil (an electric beater is a great help at this stage). Continue dribbling in the oil until it is gone and the mayonnaise is "a thick and yellow ointment."

Fold this into the chicken mixture. (If you push it into a bowl lined with cling film it can be unmolded successfully and makes a great centerpiece for a buffet).

A note from the chef

My great-aunt Agnes was, as they used to say, comfortably well off, as her husband, Billy Dwyer, was probably Cork's biggest employer at one time. She could well have lived her life without ever going near a kitchen, but she loved to cook.

When my sisters got married, with the receptions (or breakfasts, as we used to call them!) at home in our house in Cork, it was Aunt Agnes who came to the rescue and cooked, mixed, and carved wondrous buffets for the hundreds of guests.

One of her buffet specialties was the above-named salad. She usually made this from boiled turkey, rather than chicken as I indicate, but either works well.

I have adapted and adopted it as one of my own and over the years have produced it for lots of weddings and buffets of all kinds. As she was a grandmother herself (of at least fifty grandchildren), I think she qualifies for inclusion in *Our Irish Grannies' Recipes*.

NANNA'S CHICKEN SOUP

Submitted by Heather Osmon

There are no real quantities in this recipe, as sometimes you may want to add more or less of an ingredient. I'm sure some of you may not like stock cubes, but this is how my Nanna makes it, so you can substitute for real stock if you so wish.

INGREDIENTS

1 whole free-range chicken
5 or 6 large carrots
4 chicken stock cubes
Couple of cups of long-grain rice
Plenty of black pepper
Couple of cups of frozen sweet corn

METHOD

Boil a whole free-range chicken in a large pan of water (enough to just cover the chicken) with a lid for around an hour...I use my Le Creuset casserole (or "cauldron," as hubby calls it).

Take the chicken out and leave on a plate until it is cool enough to handle.

Strip all the meat off the bird, leaving it in fairly big chunks, and return the meat to the pan of water. Discard all skin and bones.

Peel and coarsely grate 5 or 6 large carrots and add to the pan (I use my Magimix, as it takes seconds to do in there and you don't lose any of the carrot juice).

Add 4 stock cubes (I use the Knorr chicken stock cubes, as I think they have the nicest flavor) and a couple of cups of rice. (Don't add too much rice, as it swells, and swells, and swells…well, you get the message. Nanna adds a whole box, but I don't think you need that much.)

Add a good grinding of black pepper.

Bring back to the boil and simmer for about 20 minutes (or 30 minutes if you've used brown rice).

Add a couple of cups of frozen sweet corn just before the end of cooking for some extra sweetness and texture.

A word from Heather

Tip: You may need to add more boiling water, as the rice really swells and drinks up the stock. If you reheat the next day you'll need to add quite a bit more water and maybe another stock cube or tablespoon of liquid stock concentrate, as it gets weaker when you add more water.

A LENTEN FISH SOUP

INGREDIENTS

¾ pound cold cooked halibut

1 pint milk

1 slice onion

1 tablespoon flour

2½ tablespoons butter

½ teaspoon salt

Some grains of pepper

METHOD

Rub the halibut through a sieve to remove the bones and skin.

Scald the milk with the onion, removing the onion when finished.

Mix the flour and butter together and add, with seasoning, to the milk, and finally add the fish.

Cook at a moderate heat for a few minutes and serve immediately.

When I tried this, I was not keen on it but some people might think differently!

CAROLINE'S POTATO BALLS

Submitted by Caroline Walsh

INGREDIENTS

4 cold, boiled potatoes

2 eggs

1 tablespoon chopped parsley

Breadcrumbs

1 tablespoon melted butter

METHOD

Mash the potatoes.

Beat the eggs.

Beat the mash together thoroughly with the egg and parsley.

Roll into balls and then cover in breadcrumbs.

Deep-fry in oil or sauté in butter. Serve warm with your meal of choice.

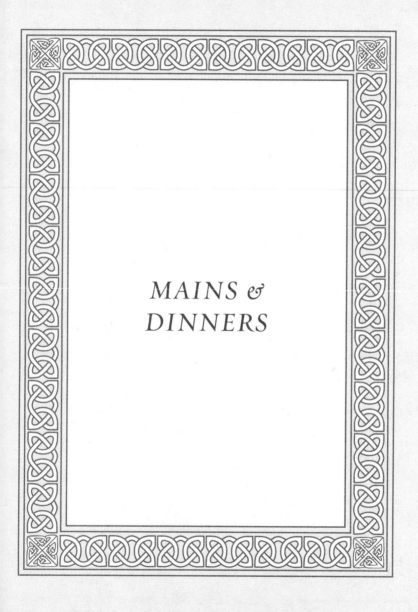

MAINS & DINNERS

JIM'S STEAMED COD

Submitted by Jim Redmond

INGREDIENTS

Butter
3–4 filets of cod
Salt and pepper to flavor
Lemon juice

METHOD

Place a saucepan of water on the stove and bring to the boil.

Butter a heatproof plate and lay the washed filets on it.

Sprinkle the salt, pepper, and lemon juice over the fish.

When the water is boiling, place the buttered plate over the saucepan and cover with another plate.

Cook to taste.

GRANNY JANES'S BOILED HAM

INGREDIENTS

1 knuckle of pork/ham

Water and vinegar

2 sliced heads of celery

2 sliced white turnips

3 sliced onions

Large bundle of savory herbs (feel free to experiment)

12 ounces bread crumbs

METHOD

Let the ham soak in the cold water and vinegar mix for a few hours.

Once you have let it soak, turn the heat up, and when it's boiling, add the vegetables and herbs.

Simmer gently until the ham is tender, then remove from the pot. Strip the skin and cover in breadcrumbs

A note from Jane

This was always served with a dainty lace collar around the knuckle and was a fine delicacy in our house.

ANN'S GENTLY COOKED BEEFSTEAK

INGREDIENTS

2 nice filet steaks

Drippings

Flour

1½ cups water

METHOD

Flour the steak on both sides and fry in the hot drippings until nicely browned.

Then add the water to the pan and allow to boil for 2 to 3 minutes.

Drain the water (be careful to preserve it for use in a gravy), add salt, and serve.

A note from Ann

Beefsteak cooked this way will be beautifully tender and the gravy will be delicious.

(Yes it is.—Ed.)

NANNY MARGARET'S PORK CUTLETS

INGREDIENTS

8 pork cutlets
Salt and pepper for seasoning
Butter
6 eating apples

METHOD

Cut the cutlets from the best end of a hock of pork.

Trim the cutlets and season them with pepper and salt.

Melt some butter in a frying and arrange the pork cutlets. Fry them on both sides until half done.

Peel and slice the apples.

Butter an ovenproof dish and lay the slices of apple in the bottom.

Place the half-cooked pork on top of them and drizzle with melted butter.

Bake for ½ hour, making sure the pork is fully cooked.

NONNIE'S CHICKEN WITH LEMON AND SAGE

INGREDIENTS

2 tablespoons flour

Peel and juice of 1 lemon

2 cloves garlic, minced

4 skinless chicken breast filets (around 1 pound total)

3 tablespoons olive oil

10 ounces chicken stock

2 tablespoons sage

Salt and pepper

2 egg yolks

METHOD

Mix together the flour, grated lemon peel, and garlic. Lightly coat the chicken pieces.

Heat the oil in an ovenproof casserole dish. Add the chicken pieces and cook until lightly browned, turning once or twice.

Remove the chicken and stir in the remaining flour mix, then stir in the stock, sage, and seasoning. Bring to the boil.

Return the chicken and cover. Bake for 25 to 30 minutes.

Mix the egg yolks with lemon juice. Add this mix to the casserole then return to the heat and stir till sauce thickens. DO NOT BOIL! (That's how it came written.—Ed.).

A note from Nonnie

This is best served with rice, a green vegetable, and a mixed salad. Enjoy!

AUNTY MAY'S NORMANDY LAMB

Submitted by Eoghan

INGREDIENTS

2 pounds shoulder of lamb

2 tablespoons oil

1 finely chopped onion

1 chopped clove garlic

1 tablespoon flour

½ pint stock (any)

1 chopped dessert apple

2 tablespoons cream

2 tablespoons natural yogurt

Topping:

1 ounce butter

1 clove garlic

2 ounces breadcrumbs

METHOD

Trim the lamb and cut into bite-sized pieces. Heat the oil and sear the lamb a little at a time, removing the meat as it browns onto a plate.

Add a little more oil and cook the onion and garlic. Add the flour and cook until the mix becomes sandy. Add the stock gradually, stirring all the time. Bring to the boil.

Return the lamb to the pot and cook slowly for about 2 hours. Stir in the apple, cream, and yogurt and cook for another 20 minutes.

Meanwhile, prepare the topping. Melt the butter in a large pan. Add the garlic and cook for a few minutes. Add the breadcrumbs and cook until just crisp.

Place the lamb into a casserole dish and cover with the topping. Brown under a hot grill.

A note from Eoghan

My aunt used to bring this to family gatherings in a huge casserole dish and it was always wolfed down! Great stuff.

MICHAEL'S ITALIAN MEATBALLS

INGREDIENTS

1 pound minced beef

⅔ cup parmesan cheese

½ cup plain white breadcrumbs

1 teaspoon oregano

½ teaspoon ground black pepper

1½ teaspoons salt

2 large eggs

Oil for cooking

METHOD

Mix the beef, cheese, breadcrumbs, oregano, salt, pepper, and eggs together in a bowl.

Break off and roll into 1-inch balls.

Cook in ½ inch of oil until nicely browned (8 minutes or so).

Serve with your favorite tomato sauce and pasta.

A note from Michael

My gran used to serve this up and claimed to have learned the recipe when she was in Italy. I don't know if she ever traveled there, but they are by far the best I ever tasted.

AN ECONOMICAL SHEEP'S HEAD

Submitted by Rose Mary Logue

INGREDIENTS

1 sheep's head
Bunch of mixed fresh herbs
Boiling salted water
1 medium-sized onion stuck with 3 cloves
Parsley sauce to serve

Garnish:

Lemon slices

METHOD

Have the head split in two by the butcher. Lift out the brains and detach the tongue. Discard brains.

Wash the head and tongue well, and scrape away all mucous material from the nasal passages.

Steep the head and tongue in cold salted water for 30 minutes and wash again in fresh cold water.

Put the head and tongue down to cook in boiling salted water. Bring slowly to the boil. Skim well.

Add the onion and the washed herbs. Allow to simmer steadily until the meat slips easily away from the bone—about 1½ hours.

Lift out the head and tongue. Remove all the meat from the bones and divide into neat pieces. Skin the tongue and slice it neatly.

Arrange the meat and tongue in center of a hot dish and garnish with slices of lemon.

A note from Rose Mary

This recipe comes from *All In the Cooking*, Book 1, which was the recommended text for home economics in 1961. The recipe gives much disgusted amusement to young people but may be useful if food prices continue to climb.

GEORGE'S GRANNY'S COTTAGE PIE

Submitted by George

INGREDIENTS

1 tablespoon lard

10 ounces diced onions

10 ounces diced carrots

1 pound cooked and shredded roast beef

2 tablespoons flour

1 pint beef stock

1 teaspoon chopped parsley

1 teaspoon thyme leaves

Salt and freshly ground pepper

For the mash:

1 pound starchy potatoes

¼ pint whole milk

2 ounces butter

Salt and pepper

METHOD

Heat the lard in a large frying pan. Toss the diced vegetables in the fat and cook for 10 minutes, or until softened but not colored. Remove vegetables and add the meat. Toss over high heat to sear.

Add the flour to the meat and cook gently for about 2 or 3 minutes. Gradually blend in the stock. Bring to a boil, stirring from time to time. Return the vegetables to the pan and add the parsley and thyme. Season with salt and pepper and then leave to simmer, covered, for an hour or until the meat is very tender. Leave to cool.

Now make the mashed potatoes. Place the washed, but not peeled, potatoes in a large pan and cover with water.

Bring to the boil then tip half the water out, return to the heat and simmer for around 45 minutes to 1 hour or until soft.

Heat the milk in a small saucepan but do not allow to boil.

Peel the potatoes while still hot and return to the pan, mash, and then beat in the milk and butter gradually. Season well.

Put the meat in a large casserole dish and cover with the mashed potatoes. Bake in a preheated oven at 350°F for around 30 minutes or until golden and crisp.

A note from George

This is a great winter warmer, which for me brings back many childhood memories of eating at my Granny's kitchen table. A wonderful time to look back on.

I hope you enjoy this recipe as much as I do.

A TRADITIONAL
DUBLIN CODDLE

Submitted by Sharon Collins from Meath

INGREDIENTS

5–6 potatoes, peeled and sliced into ⅛-inch slices

1 or 2 onions, sliced thinly

8 good quality sausages

8 rashers of bacon

Chopped parsley

Water, usually around a pint

METHOD

In a heavy-bottomed saucepan, layer the potato, then the onion and sausage and bacon, until all the ingredients are used up, finishing with a layer of potato and parsley.

Then, carefully pour in a pint of water and put on the heat. Never boil a coddle!

Heat it slowly and gently and leave it for a couple of hours so that all the flavors have a chance to infuse and the potato is well cooked through.

Serves 4.

A note from Sharon

This is a traditional Dublin dish called coddle that my grandmother used to make for Sunday breakfast in the '50s, '60s, and '70s and for dinner in the wintertime.

It is best served with a heel of batch bread, or if you are a little bit posher than me you could have soda bread with it…anything to dip in the lovely soup is fine!

RAVENSCROFT
GUINNESS BEEF STEW

Submitted by Amanda Ravenscroft

INGREDIENTS

1 pound stewing beef, diced
Real butter
1 onion, chopped
3 carrots, peeled and sliced
1 parsnip, peeled and sliced
½ turnip, peeled and sliced
1 pint beef stock
1 pint Guinness (can)
3 or 4 sprigs of thyme
Salt and black pepper

METHOD

Dip the beef in seasoned flour.

Brown in a large pot with about 1 tablespoon of real butter.

Remove and set aside.

Add chopped onions and sauté for 2 to 3 minutes.

Add in all other veggies and sauté another 2 to 3 minutes.

Add beef back to pot.

Add in beef stock and Guinness.

Add in sprigs of thyme.

Bring to the boil, turn heat down to low, and simmer for 1½ hours.

Season to taste with some salt and a little black pepper.

Remove thyme sprigs (the leaves will have fallen off and will stay in the stew, this is perfect).

Serve with good old-fashioned mashed potatoes.

A note from Amanda

The chunkier the vegetables, the better! Sometimes I add in some potatoes as a very handy one-pot dinner.

VAL O'CONNOR'S SMOKED HADDOCK IN WHITE SAUCE

Submitted by Val O'Connor

INGREDIENTS

1 quart whole milk
1 small onion, sliced
1 bay leaf
Enough fish for 4 servings
1 ounce butter
1 ounce all-purpose flour
Pepper

METHOD

Heat the milk in a saucepan with the onion and bay leaf. Add the fish and bring to a low bubble.

Turn off the heat and leave everything in the pan for five minutes with the lid on.

Carefully strain and reserve the liquid from the pan. Keep the fish warm. Discard or keep the onions, it's up to you.

Rinse out the pan and put it back on the heat. Add the butter and melt slowly.

Sprinkle in the flour and stir to combine. This is the base for the white sauce.

Cook this for a few minutes, stirring constantly.

Slowly pour on the milk from the fish and stir vigorously or use a whisk.

Continue to add all the milk and keep stirring over a low heat. If the sauce seems too thick, just add extra milk and keep stirring.

Let the sauce bubble for a few minutes to cook.

Arrange your fish on plates or pile it all into a serving dish with the sauce poured over.

Add a little freshly chopped parsley for color.

Sweet sugar snap peas or regular peas go great with this.

Serves 4

A note from Val

My mum used to make smoked haddock in white sauce when I was a child. The vivid yellow of the fish made it look like junk food drowned in thick, glossy, pure white sauce. I loved it with plain boiled potatoes and tons of extra butter. I told my friend what I remembered the recipe to be. Her boyfriend, who was doing the cooking, found it frustratingly simple, but the result was, they said, delicious.

FRANKIE WOULFE'S BROWN STEW

Submitted by Sarah Woulfe

INGREDIENTS

1 large onion, cut into wedges

2 large carrots, cut into thick chunks

1 tablespoon butter

1 ½ pounds stewing beef, cut into 1 ½ inch chunks

2 tablespoons flour

1 ½ pints beef stock

2 large parsnips, cut into thick chunks

½ turnip, cut into thick chunks

Sprig of thyme

Salt and pepper

Dash of Worcestershire sauce

METHOD

Gently fry the onion and carrots in some of the butter for a couple of minutes and transfer to an ovenproof dish.

Dredge the beef in the flour and brown in the pan, a few pieces at a time, and transfer to the casserole. (You may need to add some stock to clean the pan after every few batches as the flour may stick to the bottom, but add the liquid to the casserole and begin the browning process again with more butter.)

Add the remaining vegetables, thyme, salt, pepper, Worcestershire sauce, and stock to the ovenproof dish, put the lid on, and transfer to the oven. Cook at a low to medium heat for 1½ to 2 hours.

The sauce should be thick and the meat tender when done.

Serve with some floury spuds loaded with real butter and enjoy.

A word from Sarah

This is my grandmother Frankie Woulfe's brown stew recipe. Back in her day there was no such thing as GM food, additives, preservatives, or supermarkets. Make sure everything used when making this recipe is, if not organic, at least local. It'll make the world of difference and will taste the way it was originally intended.

Frankie was born and raised in Ballybunion, County Kerry and moved to Listowel in her early twenties, and she still lives there.

STEAK WITH GRANNY DWYER'S SAUCE

Submitted by Martin Dwyer

INGREDIENTS

8 ounces vine tomatoes

6 ounces mushrooms

2 ounces butter

Squeeze of lemon juice

1 ounce flour

8 ounces cream (or creme fraiche)

1 tablespoon olive oil

4 (8-ounce) steaks (fillet or sirloin)

Salt and pepper

METHOD

Sauce:

First, get ready the tomatoes. Bring a pot of water to the boil and then slip in the tomatoes. Put the pot into a sink as soon as it comes back to boil and pour in cold water. When they are cool enough to handle, slip off the skins and then chop the tomatoes with a large knife into small cubes. Put to one side.

Rub the mushrooms in a clean tea towel to remove any compost (there is no need to wash cultivated mushrooms) and slice them.

Melt the butter in a large pan and cook the mushrooms until all their liquid has evaporated and they are starting to go brown. Sprinkle the mushrooms with lemon juice and then the flour and stir. Now put in the chopped tomatoes and bring to the boil stirring all the time.

Next add the cream and again boil and continue simmering for a few minutes.

Steaks:

Now put a pan with a heavy base on to heat, and when hot, put the oil on. When this is sizzling add the meat to the pan and brown it on one side, then turn it and brown the other.

When cooked for about a minute on each side the steak is rare and ready to serve. You should decrease the heat and continue cooking it, turning from time to time to cook it as much as you want. (Bear in mind that the more you cook it, the more natural moisture it loses and the smaller the steak gets.) Once cooked, put these on a large plate somewhere warm and reheat the sauce. When the sauce is hot, pour in any juices that will have gathered on the steak plate.

Serve with the sauce poured over the steaks.

A note from Martin

Reading in Kieran Murhpy's blog *Ice Cream Ireland* today about the search for Granny's recipes inspired me to seek out this recipe from my mother.

While my mother was alive, this was her ultimate comfort and celebration dish, and as she got it in turn from her mother it certainly qualifies for the "Granny" label.

The sauce, according to my grandmother, had originally been called Monkey Gland Sauce. It was, she claimed, so called because in the 1920s, when it was invented, there was a belief that consumption of monkey glands would increase the consumer's longevity.

This particular combination of tomato, cream, and mushrooms was thought so delicious that it could perform a similar function.

This was their story, and both my mother and grandmother stuck to it.

The South Africans, meanwhile, have their own version of Monkey Gland Sauce, which is a fairly revolting combination of every sauce in the store cupboard thrown onto a pan, a bit like sweet and sour meets barbecue sauce.

This is not to be confused with our true Granny's Sauce.

I put this recipe on the menu in my restaurant in Waterford shortly after we opened, and it was certainly the most popular sauce for steak there for the fifteen years we were in business. It was always on the menu as Steak with Granny Dwyer's Sauce.

TRADITIONAL BAKED FISH

INGREDIENTS

1 fillet or cutlet of white fish

Good-quality white breadcrumbs

Chopped onion

Butter

4 ounces milk

Parsley

METHOD

Place the fillet in a baking tray.

Cover with breadcrumbs and onion and drizzle melted butter across the top.

Pour the milk around the fish.

Bake for 15 to 20 minutes in a medium oven (275°F).

Discard milk and garnish with parsley.

MAM'S OLD STYLE MACARONI CHEESE

INGREDIENTS

1 ½ ounces corn flour

½ pint milk

1 ounce butter

4 ounces grated cheese

6 ounces cooked macaroni

¼ teaspoon salt, pepper, and mustard

METHOD

Mix the corn flour to a smooth cream with a little of the milk.

Bring the rest of the milk to the boil separately, then add the corn flour cream to it.

Add the butter and then the cheese and boil for 3 minutes.

Put the cooked macaroni into the pot and stir in the seasonings (add tomatoes for taste if you wish).

Pour the whole mix into a buttered pie dish and bake in a moderate oven for 15 minutes.

STUFFED SLIGO BEEFSTEAK

Submitted by Seán in Sligo

INGREDIENTS

1½ pounds thick-cut beefsteak

Sage and onion stuffing

METHOD

Cover the beefsteak with the stuffing.

Roll the steak and skewer with two wooden skewers.

Bake for ¾ hour, basting constantly.

Serve with a thickened gravy.

HARICOT BEAN PIE

INGREDIENTS

¾ pound haricot beans

½ pound onions

2 tablespoons tapioca

1½ ounces butter

2 teacupfuls breadcrumbs

1 tablespoon chopped parsley

1 egg

Pastry

Salt and pepper to season

METHOD

Cook the beans in salted water until tender.

Meanwhile cut up and steam the onions.

Soak the tapioca for ½ hour.

Separately combine the butter (melted), breadcrumbs, and parsley with the beaten egg.

Roll this mix into balls.

Put the onions in the bottom of a greased pie dish, then the beans and tapioca and a little of the bean water for moisture.

Lay the breadcrumb balls over the top, cover with a pastry lid, and bake for 1½ hours in a hot oven.

A SIMPLE PLAICE RECIPE

INGREDIENTS

1 fillet of fish
4 ounces milk
Parsley, salt, and pepper
Breadcrumbs
Butter
Lemon juice

METHOD

Roll the fillet and tie it with string.

Place the fillet in a jar with the milk and a little salt.

Leave the jar closed and place it in a pan of boiling water and simmer for ¾ hour.

Lift out the fish onto a hot plate and remove the thread.

Thicken the milk with breadcrumbs and a little butter.

Add the lemon juice and seasoning.

When the sauce is thickened, pour it over the fillet.

PEPPER BEEF

INGREDIENTS

12 cloves

12 peppercorns

1 tablespoon allspice

¼ pound salt

8–10 pounds middle cut of beef

Worcestershire sauce to taste

1 onion

2 carrots

1 small turnip

METHOD

Pound the cloves, peppercorns, allspice, and salt together.

Rub into the beef, rubbing a fresh amount in every day for 3 days.

Brown under the grill and cut into small stewing pieces

Add some Worcestershire sauce, more salt, and pepper to the mix and stew the meat with the sliced vegetables and a small amount of water.

TO COOK A RABBIT

Submitted by Pete in Tipperary

INGREDIENTS

1 skinned and trimmed rabbit
Breadcrumbs
Bacon slices
Thyme, parsley, pepper, and salt to season

METHOD

Stuff the rabbit with the breadcrumbs and seasoning.

Place in a baking tin and bake in a hot oven for 1¼ hours.

When it is nearly ready, cover with bacon.

When cooked, serve with onion sauce.

VIENNA STEAK

INGREDIENTS

1 pound lean beef
Salt, pepper, and nutmeg for flavor
Chopped shallots
1 well-beaten egg
Breadcrumbs

METHOD

Chop the meat very finely. Season with the salt, pepper, nutmeg, and shallots.

Mix thoroughly with the beaten egg.

Divide into 6 portions and, with a little flour, form into balls.

Flatten them to about the height of an inch.

Cover each with egg and breadcrumbs and then shallow-fry for about 15 minutes.

CORMAC'S SAVORY SAUSAGE

INGREDIENTS

1 pound finely minced pork or beef

A little onion

Pepper, salt, and herbs to season

1 beaten egg

METHOD

Mix together all the ingredients.

Roll into a single string and secure in a clean, floured cloth, tied at both ends.

Boil in a large pot for 2 hours.

Serve hot, covered with gravy or tomato sauce.

MASHED TRIPE

INGREDIENTS

1 pint milk

2 teaspoons flour

1 ounce butter

1 onion, diced

1 tripe

Parsley, for garnish

METHOD

Add the milk, flour, and butter to a pot over the heat and allow to thicken.

Add the onion and the tripe cut into strips, allow to simmer for 45 minutes.

Serve garnished with parsley.

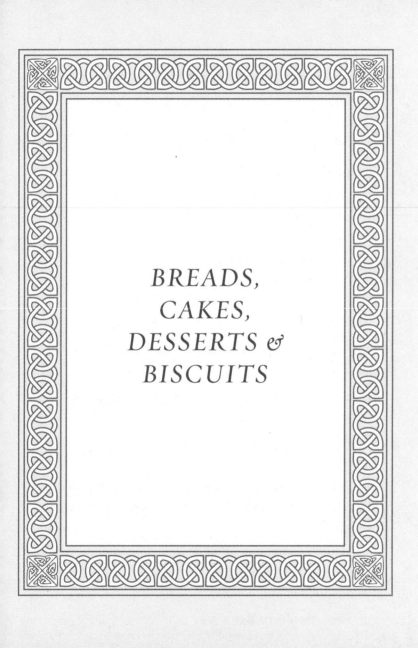

BREADS,
CAKES,
DESSERTS &
BISCUITS

ANGIE'S BUTTER COOKIES

INGREDIENTS

1 pound self-rising flour

¾ pound brown sugar

¾ pound butter

1 egg

½ teaspoon of cinnamon

Touch of allspice

METHOD

Mix the ingredients together thoroughly and shape into cookies.

Bake in a hot oven (400°F), removing as soon as they are golden brown.

A note from Angie

Don't worry if the cookies are soft when they are removed. Place them on a wire rack once they are cool enough, and they will firm up.

OLD-FASHIONED SODA SCONES

INGREDIENTS

8 ounces all-purpose flour

½ teaspoon cream of tartar

½ teaspoon salt

½ teaspoon baking soda

½ pint buttermilk

METHOD

Preheat the oven to 425°F.

Mix the dry ingredients well together.

Form into a dough using the buttermilk.

Knead gently on a floured board before rolling out thinly.

Cut into small rounds.

Bake on one side for five minutes, then turn and bake for another five on the other.

QUEEN OF COLD PUDDINGS

INGREDIENTS

1 pint milk

½ pint breadcrumbs

2 egg yolks, beaten well

Sugar to taste

Zest of 1 lemon

2 egg whites, beaten well

Powdered sugar

Strawberry or raspberry jam

METHOD

Mix the milk, breadcrumbs, yolks, sugar, and lemon zest together.

Bake at a low heat (220°F) until firm.

Whip the egg whites and powdered sugar until stiff.

When the base is cooked, spread the jam across the top.

Place the stiffened egg white mix over the pudding and return the cake to the oven at a medium heat until the topping is baked to taste.

A note from Queenie

Some people like this browned, but I love it nicely white and moist. It is really excellent.

UNCLE FRANK'S LEMON CAKE

INGREDIENTS

4 egg yolks
1 cup superfine sugar
4 egg whites
2 cups of sifted flour
Grated zest of 1 large lemon

METHOD

Beat the egg yolks and mix in the superfine sugar.

Once this is thoroughly mixed, add the egg whites and beat until it forms a stiff froth.

Beat in the sifted flour and lemon.

Pour into a greaseproof, paper-lined cake tin and bake in a hot oven for ½ hour.

OLD-STYLE RICE CUSTARD

INGREDIENTS

1 cup cooked rice (Pearl rice makes the best type)

1 pint hot milk

2 tablespoons sugar

2 egg yolks

2 egg whites, beaten

1 teaspoon vanilla

METHOD

Mix the rice and hot milk.

In a separate bowl mix the sugar and egg yolks.

Add the two mixes together, mixing until creamy.

When the mix cools, add in the beaten egg whites and the vanilla.

Leave to set, then serve.

MOTHER'S PUDDING

INGREDIENTS

8 ounces finely chopped suet

12 ounces flour

4 ounces ground rice

4 ounces confectioner's sugar

3 ounces raspberry or strawberry jam

1 tablespoon lemon juice

1 teaspoon baking soda

Enough milk to make a paste

METHOD

Chop the suet finely and add the other ingredients, except the milk.

Mix into a fine paste using the milk

Pour into a mold and steam for about 30 minutes.

GRANNY SULLIVAN'S MYSTERY STEAM CAKE

INGREDIENTS

4 ounces butter

4 ounces sugar

4 ounces marmalade

4 ounces flour

1 teaspoon baking powder

2 eggs

METHOD

Beat the butter to a cream.

Mix in the other ingredients, with the eggs last.

When mixed pour into a well-buttered dish and steam for 1½ hours.

A Note from the cook

Granny Sullivan cooked this for years without revealing the recipe. I'm glad she finally did.

QUEEN CAKES

INGREDIENTS

½ pound confectioner's sugar

½ pound currants

½ pound butter

½ pound all-purpose flour

4 eggs

METHOD

Mix the dry ingredients together.

Add the eggs and mix thoroughly.

Place a nice amount in paper cases and dust with sugar.

Bake in a hot oven for about ½ hour.

GRANNY NEVIN'S BATTER PUDDING

INGREDIENTS

4 eggs

6 ounces flour

Pinch of salt

1 pint milk

Apricot jam to serve

METHOD

Beat the eggs together, then gradually add the flour and salt.

Add the milk and then pour the mixture into a butter-lined ovenproof dish.

Bake for about ¾ of an hour in a hot oven.

Serve with apricot jam.

AUNTY MARGARET'S BROWN BREAD

INGREDIENTS

1 pound coarse brown flour

12 ounces white flour

2 teaspoons baking soda

1 teaspoon salt

1 teaspoon brown sugar

1 pint buttermilk

METHOD

Mix the dry ingredients.

Add the buttermilk.

Shape in a 2-pound loaf tin (mix should make at least one).

Cook at 350°F for 35 minutes.

A note from Margaret

If not fully done, remove from tin, turn, and cook for another 10 minutes.

OLD-FASHIONED BREAD PUDDING

Submitted by Margaret Mary Mullarkey from Mayo

INGREDIENTS

Some stale white bread
Butter or margarine for spreading
1 cup currants or raisins
2 medium eggs
¼ pint fresh milk

METHOD

Spread two slices of stale bread with butter and lay across the bottom of a dish.

Cover with fruit and repeat the process in layers, making sure to finish with bread rather than fruit.

Cut the last layer of bread into triangles to give the pudding a neat and tidy look for the table.

When this is done, mix the eggs and the milk thoroughly and pour over the pudding so that the top layer remains unsoaked. (When I did this I left the topmost layer of bread off until this stage.—Ed.)

Brush the top layer with the egg mix.

Put on the middle shelf of a hot oven (350 to 400°F) until the egg mix has set and the bread is lightly browned.

A Note from Margaret

Mam and Dad had twelve children, of which only eight are still living. My dad was disabled due to an accident and couldn't work. I don't know how we managed to survive.

Sometimes Dad had to go back into hospital and the younger children would go visit with Mam. On arriving back home, Mam would make this for us. I don't know the origins of the recipe but I know if there was nothing else this bread pudding would always be on the table.

PS: A bit of vanilla doesn't hurt this recipe, though I would avoid the temptation to add cinnamon.—Ed.

STEPHEN'S GRANNY'S BUNS

Submitted by Stephen O'Mahony

INGREDIENTS

6 ounces margarine

6 ounces sugar

8 ounces flour (all-purpose or self-rising; if plain add 2 teaspoons baking powder)

3 eggs

A few drops of vanilla or a vanilla pod

Milk to wet

METHOD

Mix the ingredients together in a bowl until fully mixed.

Use small bun cake tins.

Cook at 325°F for 12 minutes.

A note from Stephen

These are especially nice when iced.

CARAWAY SEED CAKE

From Alice McGrath

INGREDIENTS

18 ounces all-purpose flour

½ teaspoon baking powder

6 ounces (1½ stick) butter (no substitutes)

12 ounces confectioner's sugar

3 eggs

2 tablespoons caraway seeds

Approximately 2 tablespoons milk

METHOD

Preheat oven to 375°F.

Grease and line a 6- to 7-inch-diameter round, deep cake tin.

Sift the flour and baking powder together onto a plate.

Cream the butter and sugar until soft and fluffy.

Beat the eggs, and add a little at a time, with a tablespoon of the flour with each addition, beating lightly between additions.

Add the caraway seeds.

Stir in remaining flour and the milk.

The mixture should be soft, but not runny.

Place in the tin, and smooth the top if necessary.

Bake for 30 minutes. Lower the temperature to moderate and continue baking at 325°F for an additional 45 minutes to 1 hour, until cake is well-risen, golden brown, and firm.

Leave in the tin for 10 minutes and then turn out onto a wire rack to cool.

NANA HEATHER'S DATE BARS

From Joan Mulvany

INGREDIENTS

4 ounces margarine or butter
½ cup superfine sugar
6 ounces chopped dates
3 cups Rice Krispies
Large bar of Cadbury's milk chocolate

METHOD

Melt the butter and sugar in a saucepan.

Add the dates and Rice Krispies and pack well into a jellyroll pan.

Melt the chocolate and pour over the Rice Krispies.

Cool and then put into fridge.

When cold, cut into slices.

GRANNY KATE'S BROKEN BISCUIT CAKE

Submitted by Lily and Hannah McKenna

INGREDIENTS

1 8-ounce bar Cadbury's milk chocolate

1 8-ounce bar Cadbury's dark chocolate

1 tin condensed milk

2 ounces butter or margarine

Large pack rich tea biscuits

METHOD

Put the chocolate, condensed milk, and butter into a bowl in the microwave and melt.

Break the biscuits and add to mixture.

Spread the mixture onto a tray so that it's approximately 1 to 2 inches thick.

Cool in fridge and cut to size.

By chance, I have sampled this one from the Granny Kate in question and loved it. My efforts to recreate it were not as successful but it was still tasty!

Enjoy!

MRS. NEILAN'S
RAISIN BREAD

Submitted by Helen Dalton

INGREDIENTS

1 mug raisins

2 mugs flour

1 teacup sugar

1 teaspoon salt

½ teaspoon mixed spice

½ teaspoon cinnamon

½ teaspoon ground cloves

½ teaspoon baking soda

1 egg

METHOD

Boil the raisins in 1½ mugs of water until the liquid is reduced to 1 mug.

Pour off the raisin water and let it cool.

Put the raisins to dry on newspaper. (This can be done overnight.)

Roll the dried raisins in the flour and mix with the remaining dry ingredients.

Beat an egg, mix it with the raisin water, and add to dry ingredients

Mix well.

Pour into a well-greased and lined tin.

Bake in a moderately hot preheated oven for about one hour

A note from Helen

I never actually met Mrs. Neilan—as far as I know, she was a neighbour of my granny's. However, this was one of the first things I baked by myself as a child, and it still always reminds me of my granny—the cinnamon-y aroma, the taste of the plump, juicy raisins and the moist consistency of this cake that just cries out for a cup of tea to accompany it. For me, this is what baking is all about—memories.

GRANNYMAR'S GUINNESS CAKE

Grannymar won the best personal blog at the Irish Blog Awards (along with our soon to be author, Grandad), so I thought it would be appropriate to post a second recipe from here today. Enjoy this one, sounds very tasty—Ed.

INGREDIENTS

8 ounces butter

8 ounces soft brown sugar

4 eggs

10 ounces all-purpose flour

2 teaspoons mixed spice

1 pound dried fruit

4 ounces mixed peel

4 ounces walnuts

8–12 tablespoons Guinness

METHOD

Preheat the oven to 315°F.

Cream the butter and sugar.

Gradually beat in the eggs.

Fold in the flour and spices.

Add the fruit, peel, and nuts and mix well.

Stir in 4 tablespoons of Guinness and mix to a soft dough.

Turn into a prepared 7-inch round cake tin and bake for 1 hour at 315°F, then reduce heat to 300°F and cook for another 1½ hours.

Cool in tin.

Remove from tin, prick base of cake with a skewer, and spoon over the remaining Guinness.

Keep for a week before cutting.

A word from Grannymar

Guinness Cake was a wintertime regular in our house when I was growing up. It was a good standby and stores for several weeks in an airtight tin. Once cut, it never lasted very long, we saw to that!

GRANNY B'S JAM SLAB

Submitted by Catherine and Susan Brodigan.

INGREDIENTS

For the pastry:

12 ounces flour

1 teaspoon baking powder

6 ounces butter

1 egg whisked with 4 tablespoons water

For the sponge:

6 ounces margarine or butter

6 ounces superfine sugar

5 eggs

9 ounces flour, sifted

2 teaspoons baking powder

And last but not least, about half a 1-pound jar of good raspberry jam (homemade if you can get it!)

METHOD

For the pastry

Sift the flour and baking powder into a bowl.

Rub the butter in with the tips of your fingers until it resembles breadcrumbs.

Add the whisked egg and water and mix until a pastry dough is formed. Add more water if necessary.

For the sponge

Cream the butter and sugar together.

Add the eggs with a little flour.

Gently stir in the rest of the flour and the baking powder until all is blended together.

Putting the slab together

Roll out the pastry and line the tin with it.

Spread a thick layer of raspberry jam on the pastry.

Spoon the sponge mixture on top and spread out evenly until the jam is covered completely.

(Optional extra: sprinkle chopped almonds on top of the sponge mixture.)

Bake for 25 to 30 minutes or until golden brown.

Serve as soon as it's cool enough for you not to burn your tongue on the jam, with a glass of cold milk or a big mug of tea.

A Note from Catherine and Susan

A Saturday elevenses staple, fresh out of the oven, at our granny's for as long as we can remember. She is sadly missed.

MAG'S RASPBERRY DESSERT

INGREDIENTS

1 pound raspberries (You can cheat and use frozen, too.)
Confectioner's sugar
1 ½ pints cream
1 ½ pints natural yogurt
Brown sugar

METHOD

Place the raspberries in a deep dish and sprinkle the confectioner's sugar across them.

Leave them for an hour or so and then drain off some of the juice.

Whip the cream up very thickly, mix with the yogurt, and then spread it across the raspberries.

Sprinkle the cream with brown sugar and put into the fridge for an hour or two before serving.

A note from Keelin

This works so nicely because the flavors of sweet and tart combine so well.

EILEEN'S ROLLED OAT BISCUITS

INGREDIENTS

8 ounces margarine

8 ounces superfine sugar

2 eggs

1 teaspoon vanilla extract

8 ounces chocolate, chopped

8 ounces porridge oats

8 ounces self-rising flour

METHOD

Beat margarine and sugar together.

Add eggs and vanilla.

Then add the chocolate and dry ingredients and mix well.

Roll into small balls and place on a greased tray.

Bake at 350°F for 10 to 12 minutes.

Remove from the tray and cool on a wire rack.

A NICE GINGER CAKE

Submitted by Lucy in Carlow

INGREDIENTS

½ teacup molasses

2 tablespoons brown sugar

¼ pound margarine

¾ pound self-rising flour

Chopped jellied ginger

Chopped peel

2 teaspoons ground ginger

1 egg

METHOD

Melt (but do not boil) the molasses and sugar together in a pan.

Add the other ingredients, leaving the egg until last.

Mix well and place in a buttered cake tin.

Bake for 1½ hours in a medium oven.

Great with a cup of tea. My gran used to slice this and serve it with lashings of butter!

SPONGE PUDDING

INGREDIENTS

2 ounces butter

2 ounces superfine sugar

1 egg

1 teacup flour

1 teaspoon baking powder

Pinch salt

2 teacups milk

METHOD

Cream the butter and sugar together, then add the egg and beat well.

Mix the flour, baking powder, and salt separately and then gently fold these into the egg mix.

Finally, stir in the milk.

Put into a well-greased pudding mold and bake for 15 minutes in a hot oven.

MY SISTER SARAH'S MADEIRA CAKE

Submitted by Anonymous

INGREDIENTS

2 ounces superfine sugar

2 ounces butter

1 egg

3 ounces flour

½ teaspoon baking powder

Vanilla extract

Citron peel

METHOD

Cream the sugar and butter together in a bowl.

Beat the egg separately and add gradually to the butter and sugar, along with the flour, stirring continuously.

Add the baking powder and vanilla before pouring into a buttered cake tin.

Brush the top of the cake with a little water and sugar and sprinkle over with the peel.

Bake in a moderate oven for 15 to 20 minutes, being careful not to burn it.

AGNES HOURIGAN'S
APPLE TART

INGREDIENTS

For the Pastry:

> 2¼ cups all-purpose flour, sifted
>
> Pinch salt
>
> 3½ ounces butter (or another fat if you like, but butter was the traditional one so I stuck to it)
>
> A few tablespoons cold water

For the Filling

1 pound cooking apples (I used Irish Bramleys, but the choice is yours)

2 ounces sugar (this might seem a small amount to some so feel free to add extra or, if you like a tart tart, less)

Other options include cinnamon and raisins, both of which I skipped because I wanted to keep it traditional

METHOD

Sift the flour into a bowl (the general idea is to get as much air in as possible) with your pinch of salt.

Cut the butter into the flour. (Make sure the flour is at room temperature).

Rub the flour and butter together. (Try not to heat the mixture up too much.)

When they are mixed, add the water (in stages so as not to over-water).

Combine the mix using as little of your hands as possible. The pastry should come out of the bowl fairly cleanly

I tend to leave the pastry in the fridge for a while (30 minutes to an hour)

Rolling the Pastry and Preparing the Apples

Once the pastry has had some time to cool, remove it from the fridge, split it into two roughly equal parts, place it on a flat, cool, floured surface, and roll it out, using a floured rolling pin.

Lightly grease the base of your tart tin and place the rolled-out pastry over it. (I let mine drape over the edge the second time, a wise move.)

Peel (optional), core, and cut your apples and place them as thickly or as thinly in your base as you wish. Cover with your sugar.

Taking the second rolled section, cover the tart and ensure that the edges are sealed. (I pierced a few holes in the top and pressed the edges together with a fork for that real old-fashioned look!)

Cooking

You can baste the top of the tart with an egg or milk mix if you like to get that lovely brown look, but it's optional.

Place in a preheated 300°F oven for about 1½ hours.

BANANA WHIP

INGREDIENTS

6 ripe bananas

4 ounces water

2 ounces superfine sugar

Peel and juice of 1 lemon

1 egg white

4 ounces cream

METHOD

Mash the bananas and put them in a saucepan with the water, sugar, and lemon and cook gently for about 10 minutes.

Add in the egg white (whipped stiffly) and cook for another 5 minutes.

Allow to cool and remove the lemon rind.

Whisk in the cream (again stiffly whipped).

Keep on ice until required.

GRANNY REILLY'S SWISS ROLL

Submitted by Gavin Reilly

INGREDIENTS

2 ounces all-purpose flour

½ ounces self-rising flour

3 eggs

3 ounces superfine sugar

1 tablespoon hot water

¼ teaspoon vanilla extract

2 tablespoons raspberry jam

METHOD

Butter and paper a square, flat baking tray.

Mix the two flours and whisk the egg whites into a stiff froth.

Add the yolks to the whites one by one and beat well.

Beat in the sugar until it is dissolved before adding the flour.

Spoon in the hot water and the vanilla, then pour into the prepared tin and bake in a hot oven for ¼ hour.

Turn out onto sugared paper, spread with jam, and roll up.

A note from Gavin

Although the recipe doesn't call for it, heating the jam makes this process a lot easier.

SUMMER STRAWBERRY CREAM

INGREDIENTS

½ pound ripe strawberries

½ pint thick cream

Lemon juice

METHOD

Press the strawberries through a sieve and whisk in the cream and lemon juice.

As the froth rises from the mix, lay it on a sieve, adding a little more lemon juice if no more froth is forming.

Put the cream in the glasses and serve with the froth on top.

A note from the submitter

A great summer treat my granny served us when I was a kid in North Dublin.

GRANNY LILY'S FRUIT SALAD

INGREDIENTS

½ ounce sugar

2 ounces water

Various fruits to taste

2 tablespoons raspberry vinegar

½ ounces sliced almonds

Whipped cream to serve

METHOD

Boil the sugar and water to form a syrup.

Slice the fruit into a bowl and pour the syrup over it.

Stir in the raspberry vinegar and sprinkle the almonds over the top.

Serve cool and spoon the cream over the top.

A SIMPLE TRADITIONAL PANCAKE RECIPE

Submitted by Blathnaid Healy

INGREDIENTS

4 ounces flour
½ pint whole milk
1 medium egg (free-range)
Pinch of salt

METHOD

Thoroughly mix the ingredients together (using a whisk to ensure there are no lumps)

Pour from the bowl into a jug and allow to stand for a few hours

Cook in a shallow frying pan over a low–medium heat for 3 to 4 minutes a side, depending on taste.

DROP BISCUITS

Submitted by John Doyle, Belfast

INGREDIENTS

2 cups sifted flour
2 teaspoons baking powder
1½ cups milk
Pinch of salt

METHOD

Beat all the ingredients together quickly.

Drop spoonfuls of the mixture into a buttered pan from a height, leaving room for the biscuits to spread.

Bake in a hot oven for about 5 minutes (more if required).

Serve hot and buttered.

A note from John

Great with golden syrup and tea on a winter's evening.

MARGARET HEALY'S "FATLESS" SPONGE CAKE

Submitted by Blathnaid Healy, with plenty of help from Margaret Maguire and Ann Healy's notes

INGREDIENTS

Butter/margarine for greasing tins
2 (7-inch) tins
Greaseproof paper
4 ounces superfine sugar
3 large eggs
Hot water
4 ounces self-rising flour
Pinch of salt
1 tablespoon hot water

METHOD

Preheat oven to 450°F.

Melt the butter/margarine and brush the base of the tins well. Line them with greaseproof paper and brush the paper and the sides of the tins with butter.

Put the sugar into a bowl and crack the three eggs in. Place over a bowl or pot of hot, but not boiling, water. Beat with an electric hand beater at a fairly high setting. Move the hand beater around in the bowl to incorporate as much air as possible. Beat until the mixture triples in volume. This could take around five minutes. To check if the mixture is at the right consistency: turn the mixer off, hold the beaters up, and let the mixture fall back into the bowl. If it is stiff enough to hold its shape for a few seconds, it is ready.

Take the bowl with the mixture off the hot water.

Sift the self-rising flour and pinch of salt into the mixture and fold in with a metal spoon. Add the tablespoon of hot water and fold in again with metal spoon.

Pour the mixture into the two 7-inch metal tins, distributing it evenly. Place both tins on the same shelf in the middle of the oven.

Bake for 12 to 15 minutes.

To check if cooked, poke through with a skewer. If it comes out clean, with no mixture on it, take the cakes out of the oven and cool on wire racks in tins.

When cooled, remove from tins and carefully remove the greaseproof paper. (This is why greasing the tins well is so important.)

Sandwich together with jam or add some whipped cream for a nonfat, special occasion! Dust with sifted confectioner's sugar to finish.

Granny's tip

Get all your ingredients and equipment ready before you start, as you need to move quickly with this recipe to get the best result.

EVE'S PUDDING

INGREDIENTS

4 ounces margarine

4 ounces superfine sugar

2 eggs

6 ounces flour

½ teaspoon baking powder

3 cooking apples (medium size)

2 ounces granulated sugar

METHOD

Beat the margarine and superfine sugar till soft and fluffy.

Add the beaten eggs—slowly.

Add the sifted flour, to which the baking powder has been added.

Have the apples peeled, cored, and sliced.

Stew the apples with the granulated sugar until half-cooked.

Put into the greased pie dish and allow to cool.

Put the margarine and sugar mixture on top when apples are cold.

Bake in a moderate oven for 40 to 45 minutes.

Sprinkle some superfine sugar on top and serve with custard or fresh cream.

CHOCOLATE ÉCLAIRS

INGREDIENTS

3 ounces butter

½ pint water

4 ounces sifted flour, to which a pinch of salt has been added

3 eggs

Whipped cream for filling

Chocolate icing or melted chocolate for top

METHOD

Boil the butter and water together.

Throw in all the flour together.

Remove from heat, beat until mixture is very smooth and leaves the side of the saucepan.

Allow to cool.

Add the eggs, one at a time.

Put into a large piping bag and pipe onto a baking tray or spoon mixture into éclair tins.

Bake in a hot oven until firm and well dried-out in center (about 30 minutes).

Cool on a wire tray.

Fill centers with whipped sweetened cream.

Ice top with chocolate.

APPLE BRACK

INGREDIENTS

1 pound cooking apples

½ pound brown sugar

½ pound margarine

1 teaspoon baking powder

2 large eggs

12 ounces all-purpose flour or 6 ounces all-purpose and
6 ounces whole wheat flour

2 teaspoons mixed spice

½ pound raisins

½ pounds sultanas

¼ pound cherries (if liked)

¼ pound chopped walnuts

METHOD

Stew the apples with the sugar and water until soft.

Add the margarine to the apples and stir until melted.

Put aside to get cool.

Stir in the baking powder, beaten eggs, and sifted flour and spice.

Stir in the rest of the ingredients.

Line 2 loaf tins with greased greaseproof or baking paper.

Divide mixture between the tins and bake in a preheated 300°F oven at for 1½ to 2 hours.

INDEX